Fr Lorenzo Quadri & Fr Lorenzo Testa

HANDBOOK
FOR Altar Servers

Illustrated by Bruno Dolif
& Translated by Matthew Sherry

Name

Surname

CONTENTS

The Server-Explorer 7
A New Superhero: The Server-Explorer! 7

The Server-Explorer in Action
The Mass 13

Stage One: Introductory Rites 14
Finding your way 14
Entrance 14
Gathering 14
Coming before the Lord 14
Reference points 15
What now? 17

Stage Two: The Liturgy Of The Word 18
Finding your way 18
The Lord is present and speaks 18
We are a listening community 18
We are a community that praises, responds, and prays ... 19
Reference points 19
What now? 21

Stage Three: The Liturgy of the Eucharist
and Communion Rite 23
Finding your way 23
The heart of the celebration 23
Thanksgiving 23
The bread and wine 24
The breaking of the bread 25
Brothers and sisters, children of the same Father 26
Reference points 26
Presentation of the gifts 27
Eucharistic Prayer 28
Communion Rite 31
What now? 33

Stage Four: Concluding Rites 37
Finding your way 38
Treasuring in our hearts what we have received 38
We are blessed by the Lord 38
We are dismissed with a job to do 38
Reference points 39
What now? 40

Suiting Up 41
Liturgical Garments 41
Amice, Alb, Cincture, Suplice, Tunic 42
Cassock, Chasuble, Fiddle-Backed "Roman" Chasuble,
　　Dalmatic, Stole 43
Cope, Humeral Veil, Mitre, Crosier. 44
Liturgical Colours **44**
White 44
Red 45
Green 45
Purple 45
Black 45
Liturgical Objects **46**
Cruets, Jug, Chalice, Paten, Ciborium, ... 46
Monstrance, Processional Cross, Aspergillum,
　　Holy water Bucket, Candlesticks,
　　Incense Boat, Thurible. 47
Corporal, Lavabo Towel, Pall, Purificator 48
The Liturgical Books. **48**
Book of the Gospels. 48
Lectionary 48
Missal. 49
Ritual Books. 49

Training Explorers 50

The Expedition Leader 53
Travelling with an expert guide: your priest!. 54

Published 2015 by The Incorporated Catholic Truth Society, 40-46 Harleyford Road London SE11 5AY Tel: 020 7620 0042 Fax: 020 7640 0046. This English Language edition Copyright © 2015 The Incorporated Catholic Truth Society.

Translated from the original Italian Edition Vademecum del Chierichetto published by Edizioni San Paolo, Piazza Soncino, 5 – 20092 Cinisello Balsamo (Milan) Italy. Text and illustrations copyright © EDIZIONI SAN PAOLO s.r.l., 2014.

The Server-Explorer

A NEW SUPERHERO: THE SERVER-EXPLORER!

Backpacks and helmets on, rope, map, and torch! Don't worry - you're not reading the wrong book. This is not a survival course, but the beginning of a great adventure, just like the one in the novel *A Journey to the Centre of the Earth*. I'm sure you know the story, but let me refresh your memory: Professor Otto Lidenbrock finds a manuscript with a coded message written in runic characters. His nephew Axel deciphers it and

they set off on a wonderful adventure that will take them to the centre of the earth, with the help of their guide, Hans.

We're also going on a fascinating journey, not to the centre of the earth, **but to the centre of the … Mass!** And to go that deep we don't just need the right equipment, we also need a lot of enthusiasm and curiosity to examine every discovery we will make together. We can't just stay on the surface, going through the motions without really understanding what it all means: that will never get us to the heart of the Mass! So then, are you ready? Our guide, Von Dank, is already here…Let's go!

In our *journey to the centre of the Mass* we need to get one thing straight: every altar server is a real explorer, and together we will try to understand how you can become one too. So what kind of person is the server-explorer? A server is always…

...CURIOUS: Has there ever been an explorer who wasn't curious? Every server has been curious when seeing a friend up there by the altar, or at a priest's invitation to join the parish group. Curiosity is the launch pad for living the discovery of the Mass with joy: getting to know the gestures of the priest as he celebrates, the objects, every moment of the liturgical celebration leads directly to the treasure that is the goal of our journey: Jesus! He was the first to break the bread and pour the wine at the Last Supper with his disciples, asking them to do this *in memory of him*.

...GENEROUS: Server-explorers know that they are "on a mission" and nothing can stop them, not even the temptation to sleep a little longer on a Sunday! Generosity is the beautiful quality that brings you to church before Mass begins so that you can help the sacristan prepare the altar, set out the hymn

books or the bulletins, put out the right vestment instead of fishing around blindly in the cabinet, light the candles or the thurible... there's a lot of work to do to help your community celebrate the Mass well! Being a generous altar server means never rolling your eyes at the priest when he asks you for something, but just saying *Yes, here I am!* Just like Samuel did when the Lord called out to him in the temple: here I am!

...CAREFUL and **ALWAYS PREPARED**: Just like with the great explorers, during Mass too the unexpected can happen, and we must not panic! It can happen, for example, that the candles haven't been lit or the microphones are not on, or (the worst thing) there may be a little fly trying to get drunk in the chalice of wine, right in front of the priest. The careful and ever-prepared altar server, with a true expert's nerves of steel, always knows what to do and how to help the priest without distracting the whole congregation. That little fly has got to go!

...KIND: There's just no other way to be! This is a fundamental quality of every server-explorer. Kindness and joy are indispensable for bringing a smile to the sacristy and the church, expressing the happiness of serving Jesus in such an important moment as the Mass. The kindness of the altar server must be contagious so the whole group can come together like a football team or an orchestra where everyone knows they are doing their duty and "playing their part", working joyfully together with the others!

...PUNCTUAL: In our exploration, in our *journey to the centre of the Mass*, there's no showing up late...a server-explorer can't be a sleepyhead. You have to memorize the schedule of when you are serving at the altar and set your alarm so that you can be at church before Mass begins. This is important: it is a sign of respect for the priest and the faithful, but above all for you as an altar server, because being on time means being able to prepare for the encounter with the Lord who is celebrated in the Eucharist. It may be a small sacrifice, but there is no better way to get your head and heart focused on every moment of the celebration.

…**HUMBLE**: What does this mean? It means that as a server-explorer you embody generosity, punctuality, care and kindness not so you can show off in front of everyone at the altar, but so you can be like Jesus taught us to be at the Last Supper. Jesus gave us a priceless example of *service*: you must live the mission of an altar server with the joy of doing the simplest things well, knowing how to thank those who teach you and, when your turn comes, training new servers with openness and friendship.

The Server-Explorer in Action

THE MASS

STAGE ONE
INTRODUCTORY RITES

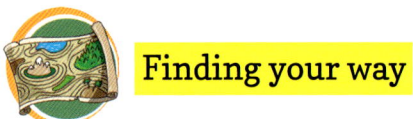 Finding your way

Entrance
The Introductory Rites are the part of the Mass that bring us into the celebration. They are like a door that ushers us into the great appointment that the Lord has made with us. We have to enter into the Mass (because it's possible to be at the celebration from start to finish without entering into it with our mind and heart) and start off on the right foot.

Gathering
The people who go to Mass leave their homes and meet in church. They come from different places, from different situations: there are young and old, there are the rich and those who have trouble making ends meet, those who are on a serious journey of faith and those who are there only out of habit. All, however, feel called and loved by the Lord; all gather and meet together.

It is essential that at the beginning of the Mass all those who meet in church should feel like a community, a family, like the Church. There's no going to Mass with earphones and standing off by yourself!

Coming before the Lord
The community that gathers for the Mass is called by Jesus and goes to meet him. It is Jesus who calls us together, it is he who is the leader of the Mass, it is he who unites all those who

gather for the Mass. The priest who presides at Mass is the sign of Christ's presence in the midst of the assembly. It is important to take all of this into account at the beginning of the Mass. We place ourselves before the Lord by praising him with our singing (both at the beginning and in the *Gloria*), by asking for forgiveness, and by joining in the prayers that the priest says.

Reference points

❶ The celebration is introduced with an **entrance hymn** that expresses the joy of encountering the Lord. When we all sing together (something that does not always happen in our churches) we feel united, like one big family. The voices are many, but all sing the same song; the people are different, but all form the family of Jesus, his Church.

During the singing, the priest and the altar servers move in procession toward the sanctuary. On certain occasions this procession is particularly solemn, on others it is very simple. In any case, it expresses the desire to go to meet the Lord. Only a few people actually move, the others remain in their places, but we are all walking toward the Lord in our hearts. Remember: this is a procession, not just walking from the sacristy to the sanctuary.

❷ The celebration begins with the **sign of the cross**, followed by the **greeting of the celebrant**: "The Lord be with you" (or similar words). The sign of the cross and this very simple greeting tell us something very important: Jesus is in our midst and we are gathered in his name.

❸ But first we have to recognize who we are and whom we are going to meet. This brings us to the **Penitential Act**, in which we recognize that we are sinners, and with humility and trust ask the Lord for forgiveness. All together, as a community, we recognize that we are sinners. We're not afraid or ashamed to say it! We say it to God ("I confess to almighty God") and to the community ("and to you, my brothers and sisters") and at the same time we ask Mary, the Angels, the Saints, and all our brothers and sisters to pray for us and help us to improve. There are two formulas for asking forgiveness: the prayer of the "I confess" and the invocations beginning "Lord, have mercy."

❹ After asking for forgiveness, in the Sunday Mass our joy bursts out with the **Gloria**. This prayer expresses our praise: the Lord has done great things for us, and we cannot remain indifferent, in silence; we must burst with joy, and sing!

❺ The Introductory Rites end with a prayer called the "Collect." The term "Collect" comes from Latin and means a collection, something put together (like a collection that is taken to raise money for charity). This prayer collects in itself the prayer of all the faithful who participate in the Mass. Only the priest says it out loud, but all of us are called to pray with him. This is why there is a moment of silence before it is spoken aloud; during this time of silence everyone should bring to the Lord an intention in prayer.

 **What now?**

❶ Above all, we must absolutely avoid showing up at church late or at the last minute, maybe even sweaty and out of breath! Before we go into the sacristy, we should spend a moment in silence, bringing ourselves into **recollection** and leaving distractions and useless thoughts outside of the church. All our attention should be focused on the celebration.

❷ In the **sacristy** there is usually a discussion about the various jobs to be done during the Mass; this moment calls for an attitude of openness and recollection. The sacristy must not become like a busy shop or a boxing ring.

❸ The entrance **procession** must be orderly and peaceful. On some occasions the cross and candlesticks need to be carried, or the thurible and incense boat. On others, your hands will be empty; in this case your hands should be joined together (and not left dangling down by your side). After coming to the sanctuary and genuflecting properly, it is time for everyone to **get into place and participate.**

❹ When it's time for the **Collect**, if the priest does not have the missal in front of him on a stand, one of you should take it and hold it open in front of the priest. If necessary, someone else can hold the microphone.

17

STAGE TWO
THE LITURGY OF THE WORD

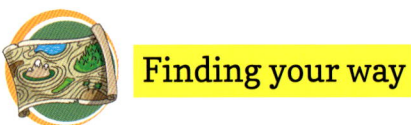 Finding your way

The Lord is present and speaks

God speaks to us in the Mass, and he does this especially in the Liturgy of the Word. When the readings are proclaimed it is God himself who is speaking. The Lord is in our midst (this is why the priest says, "The Lord be with you" before the Gospel) and he communicates to us the things closest to his heart, using the voice of the reader to bring his message to us. The readings at Mass are not simply read, they are proclaimed. What does it mean "to proclaim" something? It means reading it in a way that is clear and solemn, in order to make the words living and understandable. The reader must make it understood that he is reading the Word of God, not the words of just anybody!

We are a listening community

We can prepare ourselves by reading the readings ourselves before Mass (on the leaflet or in the missal), but during the celebration we listen together; a reader proclaims the readings and everybody listens.

It is not always easy to listen, because sometimes we are distracted, looking around or thinking about who knows what. But the Word has to enter within us, it has to be "eaten", "devoured". At the Mass, in fact, there are two banquets: the one at which the Word of God is "eaten", and the one at which his Body is eaten in the Eucharist. The Word of God must not go in one ear and out of the other, it must touch us deeply!

We are a community that praises, responds, and prays

God not only speaks to us, but he waits for us to answer. In the Mass we not only listen to the Lord, but we also speak to him, above all in prayer. In the Liturgy of the Word there are some responses to make and some songs with which we praise the Lord. On Sunday we are also invited to profess our faith, and to address of a few particular requests to God in the Prayer of the Faithful.

Reference points

❶ The main element of the Liturgy of the Word is **selections taken from the Bible**: the first reading (usually from the Old Testament, except during the Easter season), the second (from the New Testament), and the Gospel. These selections speak to us about God, about his heart, about the great things he has done (and is doing) for us, about the guidelines that he gives us for our lives.

❷ Then there are **songs**: the **Responsorial Psalm** and the **Gospel Acclamation**. The Psalms were made to be sung. So it would be good, at least on certain occasions, to sing the Responsorial Psalm, or at least its refrain. Then there is the singing of the Gospel Acclamation, with which we praise the Lord for giving his Word to us and express the joy of being able to listen to his Gospel. This attitude is also expressed by the acclamations after the readings ("Thanks be to God", "Praise to you, Lord Jesus Christ"), which can also be sung. The Gospel too can be sung, especially on certain solemn occasions.

❸ The **homily** is part of the Liturgy of the Word, because the words of the priest help us to enter into the Word of God, to understand it and live it.

❹ Finally there is the **Profession of Faith** (the Creed), which some may have trouble remembering by heart, and the Prayer of the Faithful, which brings before God the needs of the community, the whole Church, and the world.

What now?

❶ Altar servers don't have a lot to do during the Liturgy of the Word, so like everyone else at church you are invited to listen! You must be **all ears!** You must not let even a single word of what is proclaimed escape you, whether it's in the readings or in the homily.

❷ It is important to **respond** with conviction at the end of the readings, to say: "I believe, I'm here, I'm happy I have heard this word that is so important!". We must not be ashamed of **singing**, even if we think we are tone deaf.

❸ Everyone stands and faces the priest or deacon while he proclaims the **Gospel**. You are to stand with your hands joined together in recollection, in an attitude of listening. This also applies to those who are still in their places and don't have any particular job to do at the moment. At Sunday Masses, and at other more solemn ones, two of you will stand next to the priest and hold **candlesticks**. This is a very beautiful symbol: it shows that the Word of God is a lamp to light our journey. One of you will carry the thurible for the priest to incense the Book of the Gospels with. After the priest has incensed the Book, the server takes the **thurible** and moves back or even goes right to the sacristy, to avoid "fumigating" the priest and making it harder for him to read.

STAGE THREE
THE LITURGY OF THE EUCHARIST AND COMMUNION RITE

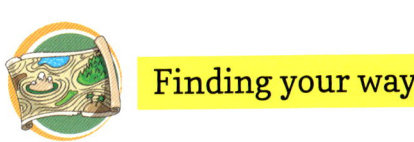

Finding your way

The heart of the celebration

The Liturgy of the Eucharist is the heart of the celebration, not only because it is placed at the centre of the Mass, but also because it helps us to remember and relive what Jesus did at the Last Supper on the evening before his death on the cross. At that supper, he gave us the greatest of gifts, the Eucharist, and he said: "Do this in memory of me"; this means that he asked us to repeat his actions in which he makes himself present in order to be with us always.

Thanksgiving

The word "Eucharist" means "thanksgiving". The Eucharistic Prayer is therefore the supreme moment of "thanks". An attitude of thanksgiving animates the whole Liturgy of the Eucharist and, in fact, the whole Mass. It is like the soul of the celebration, its breath, its fundamental disposition. In the Eucharistic Prayer, we continually thank the Lord for the great gifts he has given to us, in particular for the gift of his Son who was born, died, and rose for us. Each one of us must participate by making his own thanksgiving to the Lord. The priest says thanks in the name of all, but if we don't have our own thanksgiving deep in our hearts, how can the priest also say thanks in the name of those who are present?

The bread and wine

Two elements accompany the Liturgy of the Eucharist from the beginning to the end: the bread and wine. They are brought to the altar at the offertory, they become the body and blood of Jesus in the Eucharistic Prayer, they are distributed to the faithful during the Communion Rite. Bread is the most fundamental form of food, just as Jesus is for us. Jesus gave all of himself for us, in his death on the cross. Blood was used to seal the covenant: it was a sign of the close union created between two persons who were establishing a pact. Jesus made a new covenant with us, he united himself with us by his own blood, poured out without measure on the cross.

Every time we listen to the Eucharistic Prayer, it is as if we too were sitting at the Last Supper in the Upper Room, waiting to receive the great gift of the body and blood of Jesus; or it is as if we were under the cross waiting to receive Jesus who gives us all of himself, without reserve. Bread and wine are food and drink. You may think, that's hardly a discovery! But if you really think about it, the Lord comes to us by becoming food and drink, he enters into us, becomes part of us, giving us all his power to live. This is something great. Of course, the bread that is used at Mass is usually flat and thin and probably doesn't remind us much of the fresh bread we find on our breakfast table. We have to use a little imagination, just as we do with the wine which is very often drunk only by the priest and so may not be something we are familiar with.

The breaking of the bread

In the Acts of the Apostles we read that the first Christian communities "remained faithful…to the breaking of the bread" (2:42) and "met in their houses for the breaking of bread" (2:46). The author could have told us that they celebrated the Eucharist, but he prefers to remind us that they carried out the action performed by Jesus at the Last Supper when he took the bread, broke it, and distributed it to his disciples, saying: "This is my body".

It is an important action, which the priest performs at each Mass after the sign of peace, while the Lamb of God is recited, but often it isn't noticed because many are still busy exchanging the sign of peace. We should do what the disciples of Emmaus did, when they recognized Jesus in the breaking of the bread. They couldn't recognize Jesus while he was walking with them, but when he broke the bread, their eyes were opened and they recognized him (read the passage in Luke 24:28-34). What does this action mean? First of all, it is a sign of the unity and brotherhood that exists among all those who participate in the Lord's Supper, who are nourished with the same bread. When Mass was celebrated in the first Christian communities, a loaf of bread was taken and then broken. One day St Paul, writing to a quarrelsome community, said, "The bread that we break is a communion in the body of Christ. The fact that there is only one loaf means that, though there are many of us, we form a single body because we all have a share in this one loaf" (First Letter to the Corinthians 10:16-17). If we all eat from the one loaf, if we are all nourished by Jesus, then we are profoundly united among ourselves.

Today, unfortunately, we almost always receive communion in small hosts and it is hard for us to realize that we are all being fed from the same loaf. It may help us to think that all the hosts we receive come from a single ciborium and perhaps are distributed by the same priest (or minister).

This action reminds us that Jesus is "broken" for us; he acts like the woman who takes her container of perfume and breaks it, filling the whole house with the fragrance (see Mark 14:3-9 or John 12:1-8). Jesus does not keep his life jealously to himself, but gives it, he "breaks" it so that we can savour all the fragrance of his love.

Brothers and sisters, children of the same Father

What we are reminded of in the action of the breaking of the bread is already anticipated by the prayer of the Our Father and by the sign of peace. In the prayer of the Our Father, in saying "Our Father" (and not "my father"), we recognize ourselves as children of the same Father. Immediately afterward we are invited to exchange the sign of peace. Peace comes from the Lord, it is his gift, but it must not be kept for oneself, it must be exchanged, shared: the peace of Jesus unites with him all those who participate in the banquet of his body and blood.

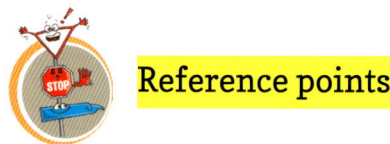

Reference points

The Liturgy of the Eucharist is based on what Jesus did at the **Last Supper**. The Gospels recall **four actions** that Jesus performed that evening. First of all, Jesus *takes the bread and the chalice with the wine*; then he *gives thanks* with the prayer of blessing; he *breaks the bread*; and finally he distributes the bread and wine to the disciples. We commemorate these actions in the four moments of the Liturgy of the Eucharist.

1 He took the bread & chalice   (presentation of the gifts)
2 gave thanks   (Eucharistic Prayer)
3 broke it   (breaking of the bread)
4 and gave it to the disciples (communion)

Presentation of the gifts

The Liturgy of the Eucharist begins with the presentation of the gifts, better known as the **offertory**. We offer the bread and wine so that they may become the body and blood of the Lord. The priest receives them, he picks them up as Jesus did at the Last Supper. For many centuries Christians carried the bread and wine directly to the altar, together with other gifts. Today instead it is the altar servers or acolytes who do this, even if on certain occasions other persons take the bread and wine to the altar together with other offerings collected for the needs of the Church and for the poor.

The presentation of the gifts is a very important action because it is the **sign of our participation in the sacrifice of Jesus**.

We always bring something of our own to Mass: the fruit of our efforts. You certainly remember the episode of the multiplication of the loaves: Jesus performs this miracle by using five loaves of bread and two fish brought forward by a young boy. Something similar also happens at Mass: Jesus gives us his body and blood by using the bread and wine that we bring. What happens at Mass also takes place in everyday life: without our contribution and our openness Jesus can do very little in our lives!

❶ Another action indicates the bond that unites us with Jesus: when the priest puts a drop of water into the wine, saying: "By the mystery of this water and wine may we come to share in the divinity of Christ who humbled himself to share in our humanity."

❷ During the presentation of the gifts a song may be sung.

Eucharistic Prayer

❶ *Preface and Sanctus*
The Eucharistic Prayer begins with the Preface, with which the priest invites those present to **thank** the Lord ("Let us give thanks to the Lord our God"). We thank the Lord for all he has done for us, in particular for the death and resurrection of Christ. According to the liturgical season or the feast that is being celebrated, the Preface declares a particular reason for praise and thanksgiving.

The ***Sanctus*** is the song that concludes the Preface. The words of the first part are those of the Angels who, according to the vision of the prophet Isaiah, before the throne of God proclaim to each other: "Holy, holy, holy is the Lord of hosts, the whole earth is full of his glory" (Isaiah 6:3). The second part of the *Sanctus* takes a passage of Psalm 118 where it says: "O Lord, give your salvation, Lord, give your victory!" The expression "give salvation" in Hebrew is expressed with the term

Hosanna. This invocation, which was also used by the crowd that acclaimed Jesus when he entered Jerusalem, also becomes a word for expressing joy, like our word "hooray". The word "*Hosanna*" therefore means: "Arise, come to save us!". It is also an invocation of joy ("Hooray"), because when we ask for God's help we are sure that he will answer us.

❷ *Epiclesis*

The word "epiclesis" literally means "invocation." At a certain point the celebrant **invokes the Holy Spirit** by extending his hands over the bread and wine so that they may become the body and blood of Jesus. In the second part of the Eucharistic Prayer, the Spirit is invoked again so that all those who participate in the Mass may become one body and one spirit.

③ *Account of the institution of the Eucharist*
The account of the institution of the Eucharist culminates with the words pronounced by Jesus himself at the Last Supper: "This is my body… This is my blood". The bread and wine become the body and blood of Jesus. This is why this part of the prayer is called the "consecration".

④ *Anamnesis and offering*
The word *anamnesis* literally means "remembrance". Immediately after the "mystery of faith" we remember (commemorate) the passion, resurrection, and ascension of Jesus into heaven. God the Father is then offered "the bread of life and the chalice of salvation".

⑤ *Intercession*
Finally the celebrant **prays to God for the living** (for the Church spread throughout the world, for those present, for the pope, the bishop, the priests…) **and for the dead**.

⑥ *Doxology*
The Eucharistic Prayer concludes with a doxology, which is the rendering of glory to God: "Through him, and with him, and in him, O God, almighty Father, in the unity of the Holy Spirit, all glory and honour is yours, for ever and ever."

⑦ *The various Eucharistic Prayers*
There are different Eucharistic Prayers. The first, called the Roman Canon, was the only one used for many centuries until 1969 when three others were added.

To these four have now been added another nine: two forms of the Eucharistic Prayer for Reconciliation and and four forms of the Eucharistic Prayer for Various Needs and Occasions. Finally there are the three Eucharistic Prayers for Masses with Children.

Communion Rite

The Our Father and the exchange of peace

Before receiving the Eucharist, we address to God the prayer that Jesus taught us (*the Our Father*), in which among other things we ask God to give us our daily bread: the bread that is our food - and that, fortunately, is not lacking on our tables! - and the bread that is the Eucharist.

We are then invited to **exchange the sign of peace.** Normally we exchange the sign of peace by shaking hands with the people around us, without moving around to reach

the greatest number of persons. We have to avoid two extremes – neither crushing our neighbour's hand, nor holding out our hand without conviction. Our act must be sincere, significant, energetic!

Breaking of the bread

After this comes the **breaking of the bread**: this is an action of the greatest importance, but it often escapes us because we are still in the middle of the sign of peace. Don't forget that the breaking of the bread is more important than the sign of peace (which can sometimes even be left out). During this action we recite (or better, sing) the **Lamb of God**.

Communion

The priest, holding the consecrated host over the paten, says: "Behold the Lamb of God, who takes away the sins of the world. Happy are those who are called to his supper". These words remind us that we are truly fortunate to participate in the banquet of the Eucharist and that we are going to receive Jesus, the Lamb of God, who gave his life for us. We recognize that we are unworthy of so great a gift, but we know that Jesus makes us ready to receive this gift. This is why we say the words of the centurion: "Lord, I am not worthy that you should enter under my roof, but only say the word and my soul shall be healed" (see Luke 7:6-7). In presenting the host, the priest says: "The Body of Christ". The one receiving communion must say distinctly and with conviction: "Amen". Communion is received; it is not to be snatched as if we were stealing it from the priest. We should not receive the host in silence, but say "Amen" (and not "Thanks!").

We can receive communion by accepting it in the hand, or by receiving it directly in the mouth.

 **What now?**

❶ *Offer up your life, too*

First of all I want to remind you of an important attitude. At the presentation of the gifts, the priest says: "Blessed are you, Lord God of all creation, for through your goodness we have received the bread (wine) we offer you: fruit of the earth (vine) and work of human hands, it will become for us the bread of life (our spiritual drink)".

Jesus uses what we bring to him to give us himself in exchange. We may not produce the bread and wine, we may not work on the land, but we do our own work every day; we try hard in so many areas. We bring our efforts to Mass: at school, at home, in catechesis, in sports, in helping friends…

❷ You altar servers **take the bread and wine to the altar**. The bread is usually on a paten or in a ciborium that contains the hosts. The wine is in a cruet (unless it is already in the chalice) that is brought together with the water. The cruet with water is needed so the priest can pour a drop of water into the chalice; it can also be used to wash the priest's hands. Sometimes the chalice and paten are in the nave of the church and are brought in procession by the altar servers or by other members of the faithful.

You must also remember to bring the corporal and purificator to the altar.

❸ After presenting the bread and wine, the priest **washes his hands**. One of you pours the water from the cruet or the jug, holding a finger bowl in the other hand; another holds the manuterge (a sort of small towel). When there is only one altar server you hold the manuterge over your forearm.

❹ When a thurible is used, you must remember that the priest disperses the **incense** before washing his hands. The altar is incensed with the offerings placed on it; then the priest is incensed, and also the assembly.

❺ During the Eucharistic Prayer there is no special job for you to do. This leaves you free to live this important moment the best you can.

❻ The words of the **Eucharistic Prayer** are recited by the priest. One often gets the impression that this is a long recitation that concerns no one but him. But that's not true - **you are invited to participate**. How? First of all by listening to the words the priest pronounces, and making them your own: although you don't repeat these words, not even under your breath, this doesn't mean they have nothing to do with you. You also participate by making the acclamations that are proclaimed at the beginning of the Preface, by singing the "*Sanctus*", by the response to the "*Mystery of faith*" and by joining in the final *Amen*. In the Eucharistic Prayers for Masses with Children, more acclamations are provided.

❼ In some parishes, **bells** are rung when the priest extends his hands over the bread and wine and when he raises the bread and the chalice and presents them to the faithful. The practice of ringing bells was in use when the Mass was said in Latin and the priest said the words of consecration quietly. It was not easy for the faithful to understand exactly where they were in the Mass, so the bells were a reminder to look up and contemplate the body and blood of Jesus. It is still an effective reminder to everyone of the important things happening at that point during the Mass.

During some celebrations, the bread and wine are incensed when they are raised and presented to the faithful. In this case one of you, kneeling before the altar, will incense the Eucharist with three swings of the thurible.

8 At the **sign of peace**, in some parishes one of the altar servers receives the sign of peace from the priest and goes to take it to the assembly. This is a very beautiful gesture, because it reminds us that peace comes from Jesus and must be shared by bringing it to all.

9 At Mass, you should pay attention to the gesture of the **breaking of the bread** and the words of the *Lamb of God*. Your eyes should remain fixed, like the needle of a compass, toward the altar, observing what the priest is doing. Don't let this action escape you! You altar servers are close to the priest, so you should be able to see really well.

10 You altar servers receive **communion** either standing in the sanctuary, or going out to where the rest of the faithful are. In some parishes one of you may hold the paten to catch any crumbs that might fall during the distribution. Once you have received communion, you should make a prayer of thanksgiving.

11 **After communion**, the priest purifies the chalice and the paten. One of you will bring the cruet and pour a little bit of water into the chalice; another will put the chalice and paten back onto the credence table.

STAGE FOUR
CONCLUDING RITES

Finding your way

Treasuring in our hearts what we have received

The Concluding Rites are the shortest part of the Mass, and often there is a danger of just going through the motions, wanting to get it over with. Then even the most capable altar server may pay no attention to the words and actions of the final part of the Mass. And yet it is very important to conclude the celebration well, keeping in our hearts the treasure that we have received so it remains with us as long as possible.

We are blessed by the Lord

We come out of Mass after having been blessed by the Lord. The blessing is the sign of the Lord's presence and his closeness to us, so we may live in our lives what we have celebrated in the Eucharist. With his blessing Jesus assures us that he will be our travelling companion, always by our side.

We are dismissed with a job to do

We do not go to Mass as if it were a show where we are the audience. We are invited and welcomed by the Lord and by the community and we participate in a banquet around which we all feel united. In the same way, we do not hurry away from the Mass, running away almost; instead, the Lord himself dismisses us and gives us a job, saying: "Go in peace and bring what you have received to everyone".

Reference points

❶ *Final prayer*

This prayer is really part of the Communion Rite, but we are talking about it here because in fact it points us toward the end of the celebration. After communion and a moment of silence, we stand and the priest recites the concluding prayer. It is a short prayer and - let's be honest - is sometimes overlooked because many of us are starting to warm up our engines for a quick get-away! And yet it is an important prayer, because it reminds us of what we have just received and launches us out toward what happens "after Mass". It tells us, in fact, that the Eucharist supports us on our journey: the Mass is always a bit like a recharge our spiritual batteries. This prayer also reminds us that we are travelling toward a banquet that is even more beautiful than the one that is celebrated in the Mass: the banquet that there will be in heaven at the end of our life.

❷ *Announcements*

Before the final blessing at Sunday Mass, the priest usually makes a few announcements. These are important because they remind us that Mass gives us the strength to do our best in the various parish activities during the week.

❸ *Blessing*

The blessing can be simple ("May almighty God bless you, Father, Son, and Holy Spirit") or solemn (with three phrases, at the end of which we repeat: "Amen", followed by the blessing).

❹ *Dismissal*

The priest (or the deacon) says: "Go forth, the Mass is ended." (or similar words), and all respond: "Thanks be to God".

What now?

❶ Altar servers don't have any special jobs during the Concluding Rites, except to **get ready for the final procession**. Keep focussed, and listen.

❷ We have to go out of Mass carrying something in our hearts. We receive so many gifts during the celebration, but if we do not keep them in our hearts, they are in danger of disappearing. The celebration ends, but a flame is lit in our hearts and has to be kept alight; if this flame is exposed to the four winds, it is immediately blown out. What can we do to keep this fire alight? We should remember an action or word that struck us at Mass, and come back to it throughout the week.

❸ We need to pause for a moment after Mass! You shouldn't hurry back to the sacristy, or come running out of it (perhaps even throwing your vestment into the wardrobe without even folding it neatly). Think about saying goodbye to a close friend after an afternoon together: you don't want to be separated, and when you say goodbye you hope to see him again as soon as possible. This is the way it should be with the Lord! Pause for a few minutes, thank the Lord, and ask for his help throughout the week.

Suiting Up

LITURGICAL GARMENTS

During the celebrations, the priest and you altar servers wear special clothes, different from what you normally wear. Why do we need to put on special clothing? Why not dress normally? You ought to know that the way we dress is very important, because it tells everyone the identity of the wearer and what he is doing (think for example about doctors, judges, or football players).

The garments used in the liturgical celebrations should be beautiful and are often valuable, because they are used in a ceremony in which the Lord himself is present.

AMICE
A white cloth that goes over the shoulders and is fastened by two ribbons around the waist before putting on the alb.

ALB
This is a vestment made of white cloth, which may be elaborately embroidered. It is used by the priest, the deacon, and other ministers during the Mass. It is the "foundation" over which all the other vestments are placed. It recalls the white garment received at Baptism, which, as the rite says, is the sign of our dignity as children of God, a gift to be preserved as a precious treasure.

CINCTURE
A cord that is wrapped around the waist to hold the alb and stole in place.

SURPLICE
This is a white vestment that is worn over the cassock. It reaches down to the knees (like a smaller version of the alb), with wide, short sleeves. It is also worn by altar servers.

TUNIC
An ankle-length garment similar to the alb.

CASSOCK
An ankle-length garment, usually black or red, with buttons. It is worn with the surplice.

CHASUBLE
This is a garment that the celebrant wears at Mass. It is worn over the alb. It is roughly circular in shape and envelops the priest, extending down to below the knees. The word *casula* in Latin means "little house": just as the house welcomes and protects those who dwell in it, so also the chasuble completely envelops the one who wears it (it was originally a late Roman raincoat). It reminds the priest - and all of us - that we must allow ourselves to be enveloped by Jesus, to clothe ourselves with him and his love.

FIDDLE-BACKED "ROMAN" CHASUBLE
This has the same function as an ordinary chasuble, but is smaller: it does not cover the arms. In our churches there are often very old and richly decorated fiddle-back chasubles. You also see straight-backed versions, which are also called scapulars (versions of them form part of some monastic habits).

DALMATIC
This is a vestment similar to the chasuble, but with sleeves. Originally from Dalmatia, as its name implies, it was used throughout the Roman Empire by the second century. It was adopted as a liturgical vestment in Rome around the middle of the fourth century. It is now worn by deacons.

STOLE
This is the distinctive emblem of ordained ministers (bishops, priests, deacons). It is worn around the neck (its form recalls that of the scarf). During Mass it is concealed by the chasuble

(or dalmatic); during other celebrations it is visible. The deacon wears it at an angle from left to right.

COPE

Formerly this was a raincoat (its Latin name is *pluviale*, "raincoat") used for long processions. Today it is worn by the celebrant during some celebrations (Vespers, for example), for Eucharistic Benediction, and for processions.

HUMERAL VEIL

This is a vestment that covers the shoulders, the arms (the *humeri* are the arm bones between the shoulders and the elbows), and the hands of the priest when he holds the monstrance with the Eucharist for benediction or in procession.

MITRE

Headgear used by a bishop.

CROSIER

Staff with a hook at the top, used by a bishop. It symbolizes that the bishop is the shepherd of the Church (as you know, every self-respecting shepherd holds a staff).

Liturgical colours

Over the alb the priest wears vestments that vary in colour according to the celebration. What are these colours? And what do they mean?

WHITE

This is the colour used during the Christmas season, the Easter season, on the feasts of Corpus Christi, of the Most Holy Trinity, of Christ the King, at the celebration of the sacraments of Baptism, Marriage, and Holy Orders, on the feasts of non-martyr saints and of the Blessed Virgin. On some particular feasts white is replaced with gold.

RED
This indicates the sacrifice of Jesus on the cross, when he poured out his blood, and the sacrifice of the martyrs, who also poured out their blood like Jesus. It is used on Good Friday, Palm Sunday and on the feasts of the holy martyrs. It is also the colour of the Holy Spirit (fire), and is used on the solemnity of Pentecost and for the sacrament of Confirmation.

GREEN
This is used in Ordinary Time (which lasts for up to thirty-four weeks).

PURPLE
This is the colour of the call to conversion and penitence. It is used during Advent, Lent, and for the sacrament of Reconciliation.

BLACK
This is the colour of death, of mourning. It can be used during the celebration of funerals and in the commemoration of the deceased.
It is often replaced with the colour purple or even white.

Liturgical objects

Anyone who becomes part of a group of altar servers immediately has to deal with various objects that have to be taken here and there in the sanctuary. It is not easy to learn the names right away and even after a few years, we still hear some objects being called by a catch-all word like "thingy".

CRUETS

These are two small receptacles, usually made of glass, one containing wine and the other water. They often have a spout. They are brought to the altar during the offertory.

JUG

Vessel with handle that is used to wash the hands of the priest during the offertory, accompanied by a shallow dish. The water cruet is often used instead.

CHALICE

Metal cup, usually gold-plated, that contains the wine that becomes the blood of Christ.

PATEN

A little plate, usually of gold-plated metal, on which is placed the large host that the priest consecrates during the Mass.

CIBORIUM

Metal container, often plated with gold or silver, with a cover. It is used to hold the hosts given to the people during communion and to store the remainder afterwards in the tabernacle.

MONSTRANCE
Used to expose the Eucharist for the adoration of the faithful. It has a small circular window in the centre in which the consecrated host is placed.

PROCESSIONAL CROSS
This is a cross fastened to a pole. It is used during the procession.

ASPERGILLUM
This is used for sprinkling: it is either made of metal and has a metal ball with holes at the top, or is a sort of brush. It is dipped into a bucket containing holy water.

HOLY WATER BUCKET
A small bucket with a handle, made of metal, and used to hold a quantity of holy water.

CANDLESTICKS
Objects, metal or wood, in which candles are placed. They are carried during the entrance procession and for the reading of the Gospel.

INCENSE BOAT
Metal container in the shape of a little boat to hold grains of incense.

THURIBLE
Metal receptacle with chains attached. Charcoal is lit inside it for burning incense. The thurible is held in the right hand: the little finger goes in the ring on the lid and the thumb goes in the ring of the movable chain.

CORPORAL
A small square cloth, starched and cleaned. It is placed folded on top of the chalice. At the offertory it is spread out on the altar and the chalice, paten, and ciborium are placed upon it. It indicates veneration for the body and blood of Jesus and catches any fragments of the host or drops of wine that might fall.

LAVABO TOWEL
Small towel used for drying the priest's hands. It can be presented to the priest by holding it between two fingers, or, ruffled a bit, on a little dish.

PALL
A square card covered with cloth that is placed over the chalice.

PURIFICATOR
A small linen cloth used to dry and purify the chalice. It is usually placed on top of the chalice when it is brought to the altar.

The Liturgical Books

BOOK OF THE GOSPELS
This is a large volume, often decorated with pictures and illuminated, containing the four Gospels. In some celebrations it is carried solemnly in procession.

LECTIONARY
This is a book containing the readings, the Responsorial Psalm, the Gospel Acclamation, and the Gospel. It is placed on the ambo, the place where the Word of God is proclaimed. There are different volumes corresponding to the liturgical season and to the type of celebration.

MISSAL

Red book containing all the prayers that the priest recites during the Mass: prayers, Prefaces, Eucharistic Prayers, blessings. It is placed on the altar. At the beginning and at the end of Mass, when the priest is at his chair, it is placed on a stand or is held by an altar server.

RITUAL BOOKS

These books contain the rites for the celebration of the sacraments (Baptism, Confirmation, Reconciliation, Matrimony, Anointing of the Sick) and of the sacramentals (Funerals).

Training Explorers

One wonderful aspect of being an altar server is that you are never alone: you may have to serve some Masses alone, during the summer or on weekdays, but you become server-explorers together with other friends, within a group. It is therefore very important to have a calendar, perhaps in September when all the activities are starting up again, and set the meeting times for the group: every parish will decide whether to have these weekly or every two weeks, but it is a good idea not to let too much time go by between one meeting and another…an orchestra, to play well together, must practice together!

The following is a very simple outline for the expedition leaders, the leaders of the group, which you can use for your meeting so that it becomes something more than just preparing the rota for serving at the altar. This is how I would do it:

1 a little icebreaking **game** through which newcomers can introduce themselves to the rest, giving their name, age, and the reason why they have decided to be become altar servers;

2 a **hymn** based on the Gospel or invoking the Holy Spirit;

3 it would then be good to read together the passage from the **Gospel** that will be proclaimed at Sunday Mass, as a way of preparing for the Word of God on which the priest will preach. After the reading, there should be a short time when each altar server can read out loud the verse that they found most striking;

4 then it is time to explore a **topic** that can be explained over several meetings, or even the whole year: it could be the gestures of the liturgy, the place where Mass is celebrated, the liturgical year, the different parts of the Mass, or even the special richness of celebrations like Confirmation or Baptism;

5 then it is time to look at the parish **calendar** to see if any special events are coming up: feast days, celebrations, processions, sacraments that require advance preparation or helping the sacristan to set up the church or the sacristy;

❻ the **rota**, for which the main criteria are generosity and humility…this means that it is wonderful to want to be involved all the time, but it is even better to make room for everyone so everyone can learn each type of service. The rota can be posted in the sacristy and given out to every server-explorer so that even the most forgetful will not miss his turn!

❼ then it is time to say goodbye with a quick game or a song and…see you next time!

One small suggestion could be to alternate "seated" meetings with meetings in the church, where the more theoretical part can be replaced by a trial run for a particular celebration or by teaching newcomers the basic manoeuvres in the sanctuary.

The Expedition Leader

Travelling with an expert guide: your priest!

Okay, intrepid server-explorers: like all the great explorers of history, we must concede that our *journey to the centre of the Mass* is possible only thanks to a guide who will explain to us, instruct us, and teach us the job of altar server and the importance of our service. Essentially, an expert expedition leader who we can listen to, and look to with attention: your priest! What makes the priest so special?

First of all, your priest himself has been an excellent **receiver**: he has devoted himself to listening to the Lord who has called him, as Jesus called the first disciples, to dedicate his life to serving everyone. He has lived a special experience called vocation, and has said: "Yes Lord, here I am! I'm coming with you!". He too was propbably a server-explorer and has generously served at the altar on his journey to the centre of the Mass, as you are doing now.

The priest is an excellent **repeater**, like those that transmit radio waves from one place to another: he has received the Word of the Lord and now transmits it, repeats it with his life to all those whom he encounters in his mission. In the parish, in the chapel or in the church he is called to spread the Word of God so that all may know Jesus and the Gospel, like those big radio antennas that transmit signals over the longest distances. Not only that: in addition to *speaking* about Jesus, he repeats his *actions*. Look closely when he raises the bread and wine during the consecration: at that moment he repeats what Jesus said and did at the Last Supper with his disciples; this helps us to remember the promise that Jesus is always with us in that bread and in that wine which everyone receives at the moment of communion.

Our expedition leader wants above all to imitate the way Jesus loves people. For this reason he is a bit like a **compass** always pointing to the Lord; he shows the right direction to all who are seeking Jesus and who entrust themselves to him to teach them to pray, to prepare well for the sacraments, to play and be happy together but also to overcome moments of suffering and weariness. An expedition leader never lets us go the wrong way.

Finally, although every explorer knows how to rely on his strength, he would never leave home without a **map!** And the most important map of all, for travelling deep i*nto the centre of the Mass*, is the Gospel: which is exactly what the priest reads during every celebration and then explains to the faithful during the homily. The Gospel is the map that allows us to get to know Jesus, and the priest wants to lead the whole community along the path he himself has travelled, following the Lord.

So, altar servers, you now have everything you need to set out. Your backpack is ready and the guide, the expedition leader, is waiting for you. With happiness and excitement, then, be ready every day for the grand and eventful *journey to the centre of the Mass!*

Printed by: Orchard Press Cheltenham Ltd, UK